A Child's Book of
Parables

❖❖❖

Illustrated by
Trace Moroney

Retold by
Lori Froeb

A Child's Book of Parables
Copyright © 2003 Reader's Digest Children's Publishing, Inc.
Illustrations copyright © 2003 Trace Moroney

Published by Standard Publishing, Cincinnati, OH.
A division of Standex International Corporation.

in cooperation with

Reader's Digest Children's Books
Reader's Digest Road
Pleasantville, N.Y 10570-7000

ISBN 0-7847-1278-6

Manufactured in China.

10 9 8 7 6 5 4 3 2 1

Contents

❖ ❖ ❖

Introduction

✤ ✤ ✤

Do you know what a parable is? A parable is a simple story that teaches a spiritual lesson. Jesus told parables to help make his instructions easier to understand. He told parables while speaking to big groups of people, and while talking to his disciples in private.

This book has seven of Jesus' parables, but there are many more in the Bible. Some are about God's kingdom, others talk about doing what's right, but all of them can help us become better Christians.

The Lost Sheep

Luke 15:3–7

❖ ❖ ❖

There once was a shepherd who had a hundred sheep. Every day he took them out to pasture to graze. One afternoon, he realized one sheep had wandered away. The shepherd left the rest of his sheep to look for the little one that was lost.

When he finally found the lost sheep, he put it on his shoulders and carried it home. The shepherd rejoiced more over the one sheep he found than over the ninety-nine that didn't wander away. He called his neighbors saying, "Come and celebrate with me because I have found my lost sheep."

Jesus said, just like the shepherd who found the one lost sheep, there is great rejoicing in heaven when one person decides to stop doing wrong and turns to God.

❖ Do you know how many hairs you have on your head? The Bible says God does. That's how well he knows you! It makes him glad when you come to him with problems or say you are sorry for doing something wrong.

The Smart and Foolish Builders

Matthew 7:24–27

❖ ❖ ❖

Two men—one smart and one foolish—set out one day to build houses for themselves. After searching for some time, the smart builder found a clear spot on solid, rocky ground. Building on the stone was difficult. It took a long time to complete the house. But when he was finished, the man knew that his new home was strong and would keep his family safe from the most powerful winds and heaviest rains.

The foolish man found a nice spot for his house, too—on a sandy beach. Building on the soft sand was very easy and took hardly any time at all. He was finished long before the smart builder and was happy that he had such a nice view of the sea from his house.

One day, a big storm came and battered the two houses. The rains fell, the winds blew, and the water rose and flooded the land. The smart builder's house on the rock didn't move an inch. But the house of the foolish builder cracked, crumbled, and fell down.

Jesus said that if we hear his teachings and obey them, we are like the smart builder who built his house on the rock. If we hear his teachings and don't obey them, we are like the foolish builder who built his house on the sand. Jesus is our rock—if we listen to his teachings and try our best to follow them, he will keep us safe.

❖ Which builder do you want to be like? It isn't always easy to do what God wants. Sometimes it seems easier to do things your own way. But in the end, it's always better to obey God. He has your best interests at heart.

The Mustard Seed

Mark 4:30–32

The mustard seed is one of the tiniest seeds that a farmer sows. (It is only a little bigger than the period at the end of this sentence.) But when it grows, it becomes one of the largest plants in the farmer's garden. Wild birds find shelter from the sun and build their nests in its branches.

Jesus said that God's kingdom is like the mustard seed. It began with a very small group of people. That group told everyone they could about God and his promises. Then all those new people told everyone around them. Now, people all over the world know about God—and more learn about him every day.

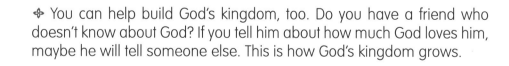

✤ You can help build God's kingdom, too. Do you have a friend who doesn't know about God? If you tell him about how much God loves him, maybe he will tell someone else. This is how God's kingdom grows.

The Son Who Came Back

Luke 15:11–32

A man had two sons. One day, his younger son decided to see the world. He asked his father for his share of the family's money and went off to another country to enjoy himself.

It wasn't long before the young man spent all his money. He had nowhere to sleep and nothing to eat. He had to take a job feeding a farmer's pigs. He was so hungry that even the pig's food looked good! Finally, he decided to go back to his father to beg for a job as a servant in his family's house. Surely his father wouldn't want him back as a son.

He was still far off when his father saw him and ran to welcome him with open arms. He called for his servants to bring his son a robe and sandals—even a ring for his finger. "I thought my son was dead, but he's alive and has come back to me," the father said. "I want to have a party in his honor." The older son was angry when he heard about his father's big plans. "I have worked for you all these years. Never once did I disobey you. But you've never had a party for me," he said. "It's not fair!"

"Don't be upset," the father said. "Everything I have is yours. You've been with me all these years and have shared my riches. But we have to celebrate—your brother was lost and now he is found! I want to show him how much I've missed him and how joyful I am that he is alive and has returned to me."

Jesus said that God is like the father in this story. He is so very glad when someone who has run away from him comes back.

✤ Sometimes people think that they don't need God and try to do things their own way. This makes God sad, but he never stops loving us. When we realize that we are doing wrong and tell him we are sorry, it is pleasing to God.

The Sower ✓B

Mark 4:3–20

A farmer went out to his fields to sow seeds for his new crop. As he walked, he reached into his bag of seeds, grabbed a handful, and scattered them on the earth. But not all the seeds landed in the same place.

Some seeds landed on the hard, packed soil of the farmer's footpath. The hungry birds quickly swooped down and ate them up. Others landed on rocky ground where there wasn't much dirt. They began to sprout quickly, but the rocks kept the seedlings' roots from growing too deep. Without strong roots to find water, they shriveled and died in the hot sun. Many seeds also fell among the thorns on the edge of the field. They began to grow, but the thorns grew faster and choked out the little plants before they could bear seed.

Finally, some seeds fell on the good, soft soil that the farmer had prepared. Their roots were able to grow strong. In time, these healthy plants gave the farmer a crop of grain much more plentiful than he started with.

Jesus explained that the seeds are like God's Word, and the different types of ground are like peoples' hearts. The hard soil is like a person who hears God's Word, but doesn't learn it because the devil takes it away. The rocky soil is like a person who listens to God's Word and tries to follow it, but forgets about God when trouble comes. The thorny soil is like a person who hears God's Word, but is too distracted by the worries of everyday life to let it change his heart. Finally, the good soil is like the person who listens to what God's Word says and is obedient. This person becomes someone who tells other people about God and his love.

✤ What kind of soil do you want to be? God wants you to be like the good soil and let his message grow strong in your heart.

The Good Samaritan

Luke 10:25–37

Wherever Jesus taught, people asked him questions. "Love your neighbor as yourself," Jesus said. When an important man asked him who his neighbor was, Jesus answered with this parable:

A man was traveling from Jerusalem to Jericho when a group of thieves attacked him, took all his clothes and money, and left him by the side of the road to die. A priest came walking along the same road, but when he saw the injured man he passed by on the other side and didn't stop to help him. Next, a temple worker walked by and saw the traveler. He also passed by without helping and went on his way.

After some time, a man from Samaria saw the wounded man and felt sorry for him. He used his own oil and wine to clean the man's cuts and put bandages on them. Then the Samaritan put the traveler on his donkey, took him to an inn, and cared for him through the night.

When morning came, the Samaritan gave two silver coins to the innkeeper and asked him to look after the man until he returned. He told the innkeeper that when he came back he would also pay for anything extra the sick man might need while he was gone.

Jesus asked the man which of the three men in the story was a neighbor to the injured man. The man answered, "The Samaritan who helped." Jesus told him, "Go and do the same." Jesus said God asks us to be like the Samaritan and love everyone around us as much as we love ourselves. That is what being a good neighbor is about.

✤ How can you be a good neighbor to the people around you? It's easy to be nice to people who like us, but God asks us to be kind even to those who don't like us. Try it. It will please God and you might even make a new friend!

✤ 27 ✤

The Great Banquet

Luke 14:15–24

There was a rich man who prepared a great banquet and invited many people. When the food was finally ready, he sent his servants out to tell all the guests that it was time to come and eat.

But not one of the guests showed up. One man said that he needed to look at the field he just bought. Another wanted to try out his five new pairs of oxen. Someone else was recently married and couldn't come. Every single person had an excuse. When the rich man heard this he was very angry. He told his servants to go into the streets and invite in all the poor and disabled people they could find. The servants did this, but there was still room in the banquet hall. So the rich man told the servants to go farther into the country and invite everyone they met. "I want my house to be full!" he exclaimed. "Not one of the men I invited first will share my banquet."

Jesus told this story to explain that everyone has an invitation to be part of God's kingdom, but not everyone will accept it. We tell God that we want to be part of his kingdom when we put him first in everything we do. When we make other things more important, we are like the men with excuses who didn't get to go to the great banquet.

✤ Did you ever have a party that some people couldn't come to? How did it make you feel? God wants every single one of us to share heaven with him. All we have to do is follow his Word.